Mastering Medicare:
Enroll with Confidence

Mastering Medicare: Enroll with Confidence

Joseph Arroyo

Barrier Island Books, LLC
Hilton Head Island, SC

Mastering Medicare

Enroll with Confidence

Editor: Rachel Bonde

Barrier Island Books, LLC

ISBN 978-1-7374076-1-4

Mastering Medicare is dedicated with love and many thanks to Bill Murray – a wonderful teacher, mentor, and uncle. I also wish to acknowledge and thank my earliest clients: Deb K., Murad and Iman T., Norma K., Renetta H., and Mike and Fran C.

Table of Contents

Preface

Why A Book About Medicare?

The statement I hear most about *Medicare* is some variation of *it's so confusing!* As an independent licensed insurance agent, I see the anxiety first-hand that Medicare enrollment can cause, and I understand why. Medicare is an important program after all; one that will lower your expenses for all kinds of health care. The plan or plans you choose can potentially save you a lot of money in retirement. You might think people would be reassured by the fact that they're about to enter Medicare. However, they very often aren't, and that's putting it mildly! In my experience, the chief problem is two-fold:

- Everyone knows at least *something* about Medicare, and
- Everyone has a personal horror story, or knows someone who does, about Medicare

These points, combined with the importance of the program to people's financial and physical well-being, create stress that makes learning about Medicare (or remembering what people learn) difficult. I believe this is not only a shame, but also detrimental to peoples' health, and sometimes their wealth. I know I have years of training, but I really don't think Medicare and its associated programs and plans are that hard to understand. Sure it takes work, but it is worth the effort. It also matters where you get your information from (that concept seems to be a recurring theme for our times, doesn't it?).

It's fair to ask, *Why should I listen to you?* Or, *Why are you more qualified than [some other person]?* My answer is straightforward:

- I am an actively licensed agent, with real clients for whom I provide education and personal support,

  and

- I write about Medicare and the Medicare Insurance landscape for a number of publications, helping national audiences understand their benefits and rights in the Medicare system

My writing, which always takes the form of educational articles and guides (no political opinion pieces!) has appeared in publications such as:

- *Marketwatch.com*
- *Healthinsurance.com*
- *Everydayhealth.com*
- *Dailycaller.com*
- *Bluffton Sun / Hilton Head Sun* (online and print, and my hometown newspaper!)

Whether I am sitting down with a current client, a prospective client, or writing an article for publication, my goal is always the same—to provide objective and helpful information about Medicare. I want people to feel reassured about their options, and that I help them understand the program better. I do not want to gain a client because they are scared, intimidated, or angry at Medicare. It's much more enjoyable to come away from an appointment feeling I helped someone make an informed choice.

My desire is for this book to provide a thorough primer on the Medicare universe; starting with the basic program, Original Medicare. Far too many insurance professionals jump right into the private options, assuming that is what's best for you. While that's usually the case, I think this approach does a disservice to their clients.

Instead, I will give you the details on Original Medicare, and only then dive in to all the private plan options available. My hope is that when you're done with this book, you'll have enough information to make a sound and reasoned plan for initial enrollment in Medicare, including the choice of a private plan that's a good fit.

If you are already in Medicare, you will be able to use the information and tips in *Mastering Medicare* to make a smart choice during the next enrollment period.

I've intended this book to be a user-friendly resource for you, one you can refer back to if you need help understanding a specific aspect of Medicare or how the private Medicare plans work.

This book is written as a dialogue between me and a person with questions about Medicare and Medicare Insurance. That person is 'you.' It will read as if I were walking 'you' through an introductory meeting. I will literally be referring to 'you' throughout this book. Obviously, this book is not truly interactive but each chapter is peppered with common questions I'm asked about Medicare. I will answer these questions *'you'* ask. The sequence of subjects is modeled on the exact way I help my clients understand and decide about Medicare Insurance.

To help you follow along, I created a short workbook (the *Mastering Medicare Handbook*) with places for notes and a guide to help you enroll with confidence. This bonus reference tool will enhance your understanding of specific elements within the Medicare plan portfolio. The handbook can be downloaded for free at allofmedicare.com/enrollment-guide.

Before we get started, I have to give one quick caveat. When we talk about Medicare, bear in mind this is a program that involves both the federal government, and large insurance companies. This means that many people are bound to have some kind of weird experience. It also means that I can't cover every single detail about Medicare. In other words, I may leave something out, something you yourself have experienced. If this has happened to you (or happens after you read this book) and I haven't addressed your circumstances, would you please email me and let me know? Send these comments, and any others you have about the book or the study guide to joe@allofmedicare.com (that's my real business email address). I would greatly appreciate it, and I will personally respond to your message. Plus, I may incorporate your experience in future editions of Mastering Medicare!

Lastly, please understand that this book is intended to be a general primer on Original Medicare and the various private Medicare Insurance options. Mastering Medicare provides a framework for helping you decide what is best for you. No part of this book should be considered advice to choose any particular plan, insurance company, or other coverage. It is not possible, and is irresponsible, for any author to make specific recommendations without consulting you and understanding your personal needs and circumstances. Please use Mastering Medicare as a tool to help make your own choice and enroll with confidence.

Chapter 1 – Original Medicare – Coverage

M

As we start off, I want to make sure you have a good understanding of Original Medicare. That's the basic government program for which most people become eligible. If we don't start there, it will be harder for you to make a decision about your coverage. Original Medicare was signed into law in 1965, by *President Lyndon Johnson*. Famously, the first program enrollee was *Harry Truman*. I think it's important to understand what the goal for Medicare was at the time as it helps to answer some of the more nagging questions about the scope and solvency of the program today.

Medicare was intended to be an affordable health insurance program for seniors, those near or in retirement. It was never intended to be a free benefit (it never has been), nor was it designed to pay every penny of every procedure. Instead, Medicare was designed to make health care affordable for America's retirees. It's worth mentioning that life expectancy was substantially lower in the 1960's, so the fact that so many baby boomers are living into their 90s, or older, was not anticipated. We can give them a pass for not foreseeing the budgetary issues longer life expectancies are causing.

Regardless of the optics of Medicare's impact on federal budgets, and on how people speculate about the future of the program, the fact is *you* are eligible, or soon to be eligible. You will have the opportunity to use your benefits, which is great; something to be thankful for.

Original Medicare is composed of two coverage types: Part A and Part B. The two parts cover different aspects of your health care needs.

Part A is your hospital insurance; it covers you for inpatient hospital stays and other services that occur in an inpatient setting.

Part B is the medical insurance aspect of your Medicare coverage. You'll likely use Part B much more frequently since it covers the more non-emergency kinds of services, like visiting the doctor.

Medicare Part A – Coverage Details

Part A covers you for hospital benefits. I think of Part A as providing 'emergency, big ticket' coverage as it is rarely used, but when you do use it, it's the result of a serious condition. You need to know, though, that Part A covers more than just inpatient care.

Part A covers:

- Inpatient hospitalization
- Skilled Nursing Care
- Hospice
- Home Health Care
- Nursing Home Care (non-custodial / non-long term care)

Something else to keep in the back of your mind is that you'll also encounter Part B charges while you're in a Part A setting. Part A covers you for the use of the facilities, and room and board. For many of the services you use while in the facility, you will be charged under Part B, which is discussed in the next section. For now though, just know you usually start using Part A benefits when you are admitted to the hospital as an inpatient, though it's possible to begin in other ways. Let's review what is covered under each of the Part A benefits.

Hospitalization

If you stay in the hospital as an in-patient, you will use Part A. We'll go into the details of costs in the next chapter, but for now, just know it does not matter how long you stay—if you are in the hospital for a couple of days for monitoring, or you are in a coma and stay for weeks or months, Part A covers this, though you will pay part of the cost.

There are many kinds of services, procedures, and hospitals for which you will use your Part A benefits. Note, though, you *must* be under doctor's orders. In other words, you can't just check yourself in to the hospital and expect Medicare to cover it. You should also keep in mind that the hospital you're admitted to *must* accept Medicare. This is a great reason to get familiar with the hospitals in your area.

While you are in the hospital as an inpatient, your Part A benefits will cover you for these services and items:

- A semi-private room (you share with others, but have curtained-off privacy)
- Meals
- Drugs you are given as part of your inpatient hospital stay
- General nursing care

- Other services or hospital supplies needed as a part of your care under doctor's orders

The standard benefit provides you with a semi-private room. But if, for medical reasons, you need a private room, Part A will cover that. You'll also receive meals and all general nursing care necessary for the duration of your stay. This is not 'Cadillac coverage'; you will have the services of the nurses who are on duty and assigned to your care. You will *not* have a private nurse dedicated to your sole care.

If you are prescribed medication during your hospital stay, it will be covered under Part A. This is one of the rare cases when your drugs may be covered by Original Medicare. Also covered will be the various and sundry medical tests necessary for your care.

Part A covers you for inpatient benefits at several kinds of facilities, and under a couple of other circumstances, including:

- Acute care and critical access hospitals
- Inpatient rehabilitation and psychiatric facilities
- Long term care hospitals
- Inpatient care for a qualifying clinical research study

Something else you should know is that Part A won't cover personal care items like razors or slipper socks, and it also doesn't pay for your television or telephone usage if those items are not included as a courtesy for guests. So make sure to find out the hospital's policy before ordering movies on-demand.

Skilled Nursing

When you look up Part A benefits on the Medicare website, it lists Skilled Nursing and Nursing Home Care as two separate elements. The benefits provided are essentially the same; it's just the setting, and the circumstances of the setting that differ. Sound confusing? It's not really, so here goes.

The most important thing to keep in mind when considering your Medicare benefits in a skilled nursing or long term care facility is that Medicare will not cover any kind of custodial care. Custodial care generally involves 'activities of daily living'. These generally include:

- Bathing
- Dressing
- Eating
- Getting in and out of bed, moving around, or using the bathroom

These are the kinds of things you probably associate with long term care at a nursing home, and are not covered by Part A. Instead, Medicare will cover medically necessary services in these facilities. This can happen in a couple of ways:

- You are transferred from the hospital to a skilled nursing facility because you need care there
- You are a resident in a long term care or nursing home facility, and your doctors determine you need skilled nursing care

Now to cover the specific services and procedures covered under Skilled Nursing. Part A will cover:

- Physical and / or Occupational therapy
- Speech language pathology
- Medical supplies and equipment used at the facility
- Dietary counselling
- Meals
- Semi-private room

Okay, now we're back to semi-private rooms! Remember, in order for any of these services to be covered, you need to be under the care of a doctor, and one of these must apply to your situation:

- You were hospitalized for a minimum of three days, and now you need skilled nursing care relating to that condition,
  or
- You need skilled nursing for a *different* condition you developed during your stay in a skilled nursing facility for a prior hospitalized condition

Confused yet? Basically, you can get skilled nursing care related to the condition you are hospitalized for, or because you develop another condition while you're in skilled nursing. Either way, the only services covered are those medically necessary to restore you to your prior condition. It's worth noting here that if you need an ambulance ride to the skilled nursing facility due to your medical condition that will also be covered by Medicare.

Hospice Care

When it comes to hospice benefits, Part A will cover these in a range of settings. The most common being in your own home or at a long term care facility. In both cases, Part A provides the benefits. To qualify for hospice care you must meet certain conditions and agree to receive hospice care. Specifically, you must:

- Be certified terminally ill, with a life expectancy of six months or less (certification must be made by your hospice doctor and your regular doctor)
- You must agree to forgo medical treatment that is intended to cure your illness. Instead, you agree to receive only palliative care

Although hospice care only provides palliative treatment and services, there is a wide range of services you can receive on hospice care. Again, these are all designed to improve your quality of life at the end of a terminal illness, so Part A will pay for services like the following under hospice care:

- Items related to pain relief and symptom management
- Medical, nursing, and social services
- Medication and durable medical equipment needed for pain management
- Any other Medicare-approved services necessary for pain management
- Respite care for your caregivers

With hospice care, you continue to receive regular doctor's care, and physical and occupational therapy, if needed for your plan of care. A nice aspect of Medicare's coverage of hospice is you can receive it at home if you and your loved ones desire this. Plus, your caregivers can receive respite care if necessary, which can be a true blessing for them.

Home Health Care

If you require health care in your home, Part A will cover it if you meet the basic criteria. The requirements include:

- Being under the supervision of a doctor, and the home health care must be part of a coordinated plan of care
- Being homebound, and unable to transport to the health care facility
- Your doctor must certify you need care for a condition that is expected to improve

Like with the other Part A benefits, you won't get coverage for anything that looks like custodial care. This means meal delivery and help with cooking, dressing, or bathroom services are not covered. However, many kinds of therapy are covered by this benefit. To be clear, these services must be for a condition that the doctor believes will get better with treatment; they are not for helping you be more comfortable at home.

QUESTION #1 – What if I'm not admitted to the hospital when I go to the Emergency Room?

ANSWER #1 – If you're not admitted as an inpatient (even if you spend the night), Part A won't cover you. You will have to use Part B benefits, which is discussed in the next section.

Medicare Part B – Coverage Details

Part B covers the benefits you are most likely to use. I like to describe them as the more 'normal', routine services. Hopefully you never have to go to the hospital, but you *will* see the doctor at some point; that's what Part B is for. And remember, if you should ever be admitted to the hospital, you'll be getting some of these Part B services during your stay. Part B covers two types of services:

- Medically necessary services, and
- Preventative services

Under the 'medically necessary' category you will find coverage for things like:

- Doctor's visits (both primary care and specialists)
- Physical and Occupational therapy
- Diagnostic testing, like blood work, x-rays, MRI, etc.
- Durable Medical Equipment (DME), like walkers, CPAP machines, bottled oxygen
- Mental health care
- Emergency transportation
- Very limited outpatient prescription drugs, including IV-based cancer treatments
- Clinical research

Most of these services are probably familiar to you, so we won't spend as much time on them, but the general idea on medically necessary services is you use them when you have a medical issue. For example, you have a cold, or maybe the flu. You make an appointment with your doctor. At the appointment, you get tested for the flu. If your cough is bad enough, you might get a chest x-ray. Part B will be used to cover these kinds of expenses.

The big exception to thinking about Part B being for 'ordinary' things is cancer treatment. This is obviously a major health issue, and hopefully not one that is ever routine to you. However, you need to know that Part B covers infusion-based cancer treatments, like chemotherapy. Part B also covers radiation and some cancer treatments given orally.

If you are eligible to participate in clinical trials for medical care, Part B will cover this if it is for a Medicare-approved purpose. On their website, Medicare gives an example of clinical trials for a new cancer drug; Part B would cover this treatment.

The other side of the Part B 'coin' is preventative services. These services and procedures are designed to either prevent, or detect at an early stage, illness and disease. The list of preventative services is long, but you can generally think of them in these broad categories:

- Vaccines like the flu and COVID-19 shot
- Cancer screenings
- Other wellness services, like depression screening and alcohol and tobacco misuse counselling

Between medically necessary and preventative treatments, you will find your everyday and year to year needs are covered by Part B. And, if emergency strikes, Part A is there for you, so taken together, Original Medicare adequately replaces private insurance.

QUESTION #2 I've heard that Medicare doesn't cover everything. What doesn't it cover?

ANSWER #2 – You're right. Medicare doesn't cover everything, including some things you might need as you age. In general, Medicare will not cover services or procedures that are or involve:

- Long-term or custodial care
- Most dental care, except for specific, and rare occasions
- Eye exams relating to prescribing glasses
- Cosmetic in nature
- Acupuncture, except for chronic lower back pain
- Hearing aids, exams, or fittings
- Routine foot care
- Most prescription drugs except those specifically covered by Part B, or when they're covered by Part A

If you use these services, then you need to know up front that Original Medicare will not cover them. You will have to make separate arrangements to obtain coverage. We'll get to some options for you to consider in a while.

QUESTION #3 – Does Medicare work outside of the U.S.?

ANSWER #3 – Basically, no; Medicare works only within the United States. There are some specific exceptions though. They mostly involve being in Canada on your way to or from Alaska. If you plan to travel extensively, you will want to make arrangements for supplemental health insurance coverage, which we'll get to later on.

Medicare Eligibility

You are eligible for Medicare if either of these applies:

- You are a U.S. citizen,
  or
- You are a permanent legal resident

To qualify as a legal resident, you must have legally resided in the U.S. for five consecutive years. The thing to remember here is that this aspect of eligibility tells you whether you can get Medicare someday *in the future*. You won't necessarily enter Medicare the moment you meet these criteria; you'll need to satisfy some other entry requirement.

In other words, something has to happen in order for you to actually enter Medicare. We called this a 'triggering event' when I used to work in the 401(k) industry. You're already eligible for Medicare because you're a citizen or a legal resident, and then, something happens: a life event, and now you actually enter Medicare and can start using your benefits. Here are the triggers that will get you into the program:

- Turning age 65
- Receiving disability income from Social Security or the Railroad Retirement Board for 24 consecutive months, regardless of age
- Being diagnosed with Lou Gehrig's disease (ALS), regardless of age
- Being diagnosed with End Stage Renal Disease (ESRD), regardless of age

We must be clear on this point. Your citizenship or resident status determines *whether* you will *ever* be able to have Medicare. Your life circumstances, like age or disability, determine *when* you enter Medicare.

Most people enter Medicare because they turn 65. For those people, you have a seven month window to enroll. This is called your Initial Election Period (IEP), and it spans:

- Three months before the month you turn 65
- The month you turn 65
- Three months after the month you turn 65

If you enroll before you turn 65, you will enter on the first day of the month you turn 65. For example, if you turn 65 in July, and you enroll in May, your coverage will start July 1st. If you enroll after you turn 65, your coverage can be delayed. For instance, if your birthday is in July, but you don't enroll until September, your coverage will start on December 1st, three months after you signed up. If you are in any way counting on your Medicare coverage, make sure to sign up before your 65th birthday so your coverage will start as early as possible.

If you become eligible for Medicare because of a diagnosis of ALS, your coverage will automatically start on the first day you receive Social Security Disability payments. Before 2021, there was a five month waiting period for disability benefits to begin. This has been revoked. Starting in 2021, Disability and Medicare will begin without delay. This makes it important to sign up for disability as soon as you receive your diagnosis; this will allow your Medicare benefits to start quickly.

As for getting Medicare based on ESRD, the rules are more complicated, and can vary based on whether you receive a kidney transplant or not. However, for simplicity's sake, you can assume you will enter Medicare on the first day of the fourth month you receive dialysis treatments. The four month window starts when you actually begin dialysis, even if you have not yet applied for Medicare. This means that your Medicare coverage might be retroactive if you forget to enroll when you're first eligible. Whenever you do enroll, your Medicare coverage will be retroactive back to the fourth month of your dialysis treatments. However, it's best not to delay—enroll when you are first eligible.

QUESTION #4 – Do I have to start Medicare at 65? I've heard you can delay Medicare.

ANSWER #4 – No, you don't have to enroll when you turn 65. In fact, you may want to delay your benefits, especially Part B. However, it's very important to remember that if you don't take Part B when you are first eligible you could incur a late enrollment penalty unless you meet certain requirements.

You can safely delay taking Part B if you are covered by your employer (or spouse's employer) health plan, and your employer (or spouse's employer) employs more than 20 people. As long as you remain covered by this plan, you can avoid taking Part B; this will possibly save you money (more on costs in the next chapter) in the long run. When your coverage ends (either because you or your spouse retire or otherwise lose coverage), you will have a special opportunity to enroll in Medicare called a Special Enrollment Period (SEP).

Your SEP will begin the *earlier* of:

- The month after your / your spouse's employment ends
- The month after your coverage ends

Your SEP lasts for eight months, and you can enroll in Part A, B, or both during this window. As long as you enroll during the SEP, your enrollment is not considered late, even if you are many years older than 65.

Many people start Part A at 65, even if they still have employer coverage. There are many complicated interactions between Medicare and employer coverage. For this reason, I advise all my clients, and you too, to talk to your HR department as you approach 65. Don't wait until you are already 65. Ask months in advance if you need to take Medicare at 65. They will inform you if your employer coverage meets the requirement to delay coverage, or if you should enroll to avoid a penalty.

The bottom line here is that if you are going to stay covered by an employer plan, you may want to take Part A and delay Part B, as long as your coverage meets the Medicare minimum requirements. This will likely save you money.

What To Remember:

- Part A covers you for hospital or other institutional care
- Part B covers most preventative or medically necessary services
- Many things you may need, like dental, vision, and hearing are not covered by either Part A or B – you will need to make your own arrangements for these services
- Every U.S. citizen is eligible for Medicare, and so are permanent legal residents who have resided in the U.S. for at least five years
- You will probably enter Medicare at age 65, but it could be earlier in some cases
- You have the option to delay taking Part A and / or B, and if your employer coverage meets the minimum requirements, delaying Part B could save you money

Chapter 2 – Original Medicare – Costs

M

You can see that the coverage you will get from Original Medicare is pretty good. It will cover most of the things you'll likely need, and even some big ticket items, like cancer treatments. With the basics out of the way, let's review the part you're probably most interested in. How much is this going to cost you?

Remember, Medicare was never intended to be 100% comprehensive, or 100% free. The program was designed for you to pick up some of the costs. We will start by reviewing what it costs just to have Medicare. In other words, how much (and when) will you pay for the right to have Medicare?

Once again, there's a distinction between the two parts – A and B. Although there is some overlap, you generally pay for them in different ways. We will start with Part A.

Medicare Part A – How Much Does Coverage Cost?

There is a common thought that Part A is 'free'—this is generally not true. What actually happens is that many (most) people do not have to pay a monthly premium for coverage. This is only true when you have paid payroll taxes for at least ten years.

If you're an employee, you have probably noticed on your W2 a box for wages subject to Medicare taxes. These Medicare taxes, often called 'payroll' taxes or

'FICA', are withheld from your paycheck every pay period. For your entire working career, you've been paying a tax (currently 1.45%) on your wages. Your employer matches this amount, so a total of 2.9% of your wages are paid into the Medicare system. And yes, there really is a Medicare 'trust fund', but don't ask about its funding status (that's a topic for a separate book).

If your wages are over $200,000, you pay an additional 0.9% tax on those amounts. Now, if you're self-employed, you pay both 'halves' of FICA or payroll taxes, so you are still contributing your 2.9% to Medicare Part A (and more if your income is above the threshold amount).

You might have begun paying this tax in your teens... let's say you started earning taxable wages at age 17. So, by the time you hit Medicare age, you've paid taxes for nearly fifty years. Obviously, the amount you have paid is dependent on your income, which probably started small and grew over time. According to some estimates, higher wage earners may pay as much as $84,000 in taxes into the Part A trust fund (Guo & Moon, 2017).

You can already see that Part A is hardly 'free'; that is, if you qualify for premium-free Part A. To get Part A without paying an additional premium, you must have paid FICA for a minimum of 40 'quarters'—the same metric used to determine your Social Security income eligibility. Generally, this is ten years of work. If you expect to get Social Security, you can be confident you will get premium-free Part A too. In fact, your Social Security statements will also show your projected Medicare benefits based on your work history.

QUESTION #1 – What if I never worked, or didn't work enough?

ANSWER #1 – If you didn't work enough to qualify for premium-free Part A, you might qualify for it based on your marriage to someone who did. You can qualify based on your spouse's work history in these ways:

- Currently married for at least one year, and your spouse qualifies for premium-free Part A
- Widowed and currently single, but married for at least nine months, and your spouse qualified, or would have qualified, for premium-free Part A
- Divorced and single, but married for at least ten years, and your ex-spouse qualified for premium-free Part A

If you don't meet any of these criteria, you can still get Part A benefits, but you're going to have to pay a premium. The premium amount varies based on how much work history you have (or your spouse has). There are two premium tiers for 2021:

- Full-premium, $471 per month
- Partial-premium, $259 per month

If you must pay to get Part A, you will also have to enroll in Part B (we'll touch on this cost shortly). However, you can choose not to sign up and pay for Part A, and only enroll in Part B. Confused? Here are the basic scenarios:

- You qualify for premium- free Part A based on your work history or your spouse's

- You do not qualify for premium-free Part A, but you choose to sign up for it and pay the monthly premium. You must also enroll in Part B in this case.
- You do not qualify for premium-free Part A. You choose *not* to enroll in it, so you won't have to pay the Part A premium. You can still *choose* to enroll in Part B in this case if you'd like.

Medicare Part B – How Much Does Coverage Cost?

Part B is a little simpler. There is none of this qualifying for premium-free coverage business. You don't pay for it throughout your working career like with Part A. Instead, you pay a monthly premium once you enroll. This is why you may decide to delay enrolling if you still have employer coverage, because once you enroll in Part B, you will start paying a monthly premium.

For 2021, the base monthly premium for Part B is $148.50. If you're drawing Social Security, your premium will be automatically deducted from your payments. If you are not drawing Social Security yet, you'll get a bill for your premiums.

The $148.50 per month is the base premium. If your income is over certain thresholds, you could pay more. These higher premiums are called Income-Related Monthly Adjustment Amount (IRMAA). These add-ons to your part B premium begin with incomes above $88,000 per year for single filers, and $176,000 for joint filers. At this first level, you will pay an additional $59.40 per month, making your total monthly premium $207.90. The highest income bracket, single incomes over $500,000, and joint filing incomes above $750,000, has an additional premium of $356.40, for a total monthly premium of $504.90 per month.

This is obviously a significant additional premium, so let's talk about when this is applicable to you. For one thing, your Part B premium is based on your income two tax years in the past. For example, your 2021 premium is calculated based on your 2019 tax filing. This often creates problems for people who receive a severance package or retirement bonus in their last year or two of employment. Two tax years later, when Social Security looks at your tax return, your income is artificially inflated and now you're in one of these IRMAA bands.

One way to avoid this is to take your severance or retirement bonus three tax years before you take Medicare Part B. If you have this flexibility, it will save you money, time, and effort. If you don't have that kind of flexibility, know that you can appeal your IRMAA premium amount. If you can demonstrate that you had a change in circumstances, (like retiring and incurring a drop in your income) you can appeal your premium amount using Form SSA-44.

Medicare Part B – Late Enrollment Penalty

Besides the standard Part B premium, plus IRMAA amounts, if applicable, you could also pay a late enrollment penalty if you don't enroll in Part B when you are first eligible. We already reviewed the eligibility and enrollment windows for Original Medicare in chapter one. If you don't enroll when you are eligible, and you're not covered by a qualifying group employer or union health insurance plan, you will pay a late enrollment penalty.

The penalty amount is equal to 10% of the Part B premium for each full year your enrollment is late. For example, if you should have enrolled by June of 2019 (the last month of your seven month Initial Election Period), but you don't actually enroll until July of 2021, your enrollment is considered two years late. Fortunately, Medicare only counts full twelve-month periods. This means that your total penalty is 20% (2 years x 10%) of the standard Part B premium. In our example, that would make your total Part B premium $178.20 ($148.50 standard premium, plus $29.70 penalty). You will pay this penalty amount for as long as you're in Part B; it never goes away.

Of course, you won't pay the penalty if you have been covered by a qualifying employer or group plan. In that case, you'll get a Special Enrollment Period to enter Medicare, and your enrollment is considered on-time.

QUESTION #2 – What if I can't afford my Medicare premiums?

ANSWER #2 – If you qualify for *Medicaid*, a joint federal and state health insurance program, you may not have to pay your Part A or B premiums. People who qualify for Medicaid at varying levels are eligible for the *Medicare Savings Program*. This program pays for some or all of their Medicare premiums, and also many of the out of pocket expenses you'll learn about shortly. If you think, even for a minute, that you might qualify for Medicaid, please apply with your State. The worst that can happen is that you're not approved. If you are approved, you will get a ton of help paying for your health care.

In the grand scheme of things, these premium payments aren't particularly high, especially if you've been paying for individual insurance, and if you don't have to pay for Part A. However (you knew there was some kind of 'but' coming, right?), these are not the only costs you'll pay under Medicare. You will also pay for most of the services you use. We'll spend the rest of the chapter finding out what kinds of out of pocket costs you can expect with Original Medicare.

Original Medicare Part A – Out Of Pocket Costs

As with the basic coverage and premium amounts, your out of pocket costs for services and procedures for Part A and B are different. We'll cover Part A first.

Since Part A covers more 'emergency-type' of services like hospitalization, your costs tend to come in bigger chunks. The basic cost you will face is the Part A Deductible. For 2021, this amount is $1,484. A deductible is the amount you have to pay before your insurance starts covering your costs. So, if you are admitted to the hospital, you will pay the first $1,484 of the costs out of pocket with Original Medicare. Like we said before, if you're not admitted as an inpatient, you will pay Part B costs, which we'll review in the next section.

A very important point to understand is that the Part A Deductible applies for each Benefit Period. This means it is possible to pay the Part A Deductible more than once in a year. This is an unusual feature, totally unlike traditional private health insurance. With private health insurance (whether employer coverage, or individual plans), once you meet the deductible, you're done. You won't pay it more than once. With Medicare, you *do not* have that protection.

QUESTION #3 – What is a Benefit Period?

ANSWER #3 – Medicare.gov says this about Benefit Periods: *A benefit period begins the day you're admitted as an inpatient in a hospital or Skilled Nursing Facility. The benefit period ends when you haven't received any inpatient hospital care (or skilled care in a SNF) for 60 days in a row. If you go into a hospital or a SNF after one benefit period has ended, a new benefit period begins.*

I tell people a Benefit Period is a window of time related to a *specific* hospitalization or skilled nursing visit. As long as you keep receiving covered services (like staying in the hospital or getting skilled nursing care), you stay in your Benefit Period and you only pay the deductible once. However, once you go sixty days *without* receiving Part A covered services, you will start a new Benefit Period if you have to go back to the hospital or skilled nursing facility.

Besides the Part A Deductible, you could be on the hook for other out of pocket costs with Part A. When you're admitted to the hospital or skilled nursing, you will pay the deductible. Once you've paid that, you're covered for:

- Up to sixty days in the hospital, for $0 copay per day
- Up to twenty days in skilled nursing, for $0 copay per day

This is a pretty good deal – up to sixty days in the hospital or up to twenty days in skilled nursing for $1,484. You could even do both, stay in the hospital for sixty days, and get twenty days of skilled nursing, all in the same benefit period, and pay just the $1,484 in Part A costs.

If you have a severe illness and you need to stay in the hospital beyond sixty days, or if you need more than twenty days of skilled nursing care, you will incur more out of pocket costs. Now you'll have to pay:

- $352 per day for hospital stays between sixty-one and ninety days, and
- $185.50 per day for skilled nursing stays between twenty-one and one hundred days.

This can add up over time, depending on the length of your stay. There's more though. If you need more care than this, you will face these costs:

- $704 per day for hospital stays longer than ninety days, as long as you have Lifetime Reserve Days left (we'll get to this in a second)
- Full cost for skilled nursing care beyond one hundred days (there are no Lifetime Reserve Days for skilled nursing care)

And lastly, if you should use up all of your Lifetime Reserve Days, and need to be in the hospital beyond ninety days, you will pay the full cost out of pocket.

QUESTION #4 – What are Lifetime Reserve Days?

ANSWER #4 – Lifetime Reserve Days are extra days of coverage available for every Part A beneficiary. You are given a total of ninety, and once they're gone, they're gone. Note though, you only use a Lifetime Reserve Day once you've had more than ninety days in the hospital *during a single benefit period.* If you are in the hospital for sixty days in June, and then sixty more in September, you're not using Lifetime Reserve Days as long as you are in a new Benefit Period; instead, you'll pay the Part A Deductible again. If your second stay lasts more than sixty days, you will pay the daily co-payment until your second stay exceeds ninety days. Only then will you start using Lifetime Reserve Days, if you have any left. Again, the important thing to remember is that you will only use a Lifetime Reserve Day once you've had a *single stay* longer than ninety days. Medicare doesn't keep track of your stays of less than ninety days and add them together. You must exceed ninety consecutive days to begin using your Lifetime Reserve Days.

An even more important thing to remember is that *with Original Medicare, there is no cap on your out of pocket costs.* We will return to this once we've talked about your costs under Part B, but I want to bring it up right now to get you thinking about it, because it may be the most important fact about Medicare you need to know.

Original Medicare Part B – Out Of Pocket Costs

Your costs under Original Medicare Part B are simpler. You have two basic costs:

- Part B Deductible ($203 for 2021), and

- Part B co-insurance (20% of the Medicare-approved charges for most services and procedures)

Just to make sure you're good and confused, you only pay the Part B Deductible ($203) once during the year. This makes it *unlike* the Part A Deductible, and *more like* regular private health insurance. You will pay the first $203 for Part B medical services before Medicare begins covering part of your costs. Once you've paid the full $203, you're done with the deductible until January of the next year—it's truly an annual deductible.

Once you've met the Part B Deductible, then Medicare will cover 80% of the Medicare-approved cost for your Part B services and procedures. You will pay the other 20% of the cost. You'll do this for every service and procedure you use during the year.

Once again, you need to know with Original Medicare, *there is no cap on your out of pocket costs each year*. This is also very different from any other kind of health insurance you're used to having. Individual or employer group health insurance has an Out Of Pocket Maximum (OOPM) cap. Once you've hit your OOPM, a non-Medicare plan covers 100% of your eligible expenses for the rest of the year. Medicare is not like that. You keep paying your 20% Part B co-insurance and Part A Deductible and co-insurance throughout the year, no matter how much you've already spent.

One other expense you need to know about is Part B Excess Charges. These charges can be up to 15% of the Medicare-approved amount, and they are added to your 20% co-insurance. This means that if you have to pay Excess Charges, your total out of pocket cost could be 35%. So, what are Excess Charges? Excess Charges are amounts some providers charge above and beyond Medicare's approved prices. Most providers accept Medicare *Assignment*, which means they have agreed to accept Medicare's prices as payment-in-full. If a provider doesn't accept Assignment, then they still receive Medicare's standard reimbursement, but they are allowed to add up to 15% as an Excess Charge, which you pay.

Medicare makes Assignment attractive to providers by paying them more than providers who don't accept Assignment. Providers who accept Assignment receive 5% more from Medicare. For this and other reasons, most physicians and facilities agree to accept Medicare Assignment. However, some do not, and those are the ones who can charge the additional 15%. The good news is you can always find out ahead of time if your provider accepts Assignment. If they don't, you can find one who does, or just understand that you will be responsible for an additional 15% charge on their Part B services.

So, what does it all add up to? You can count on paying the Part B Deductible every year, and though it is much less than the Part A Deductible, it goes up each year. You can also count on paying 20% co-insurance for most Part B services and procedures.

QUESTION #5 – Can you give me an example of Part B expenses?

ANSWER #5 – Here are three hypothetical situations showing how Part B pricing works:

Example #1 – You go to the doctor (who accepts Medicare Assignment) because you think you have the flu. You receive a flu test and a chest x-ray while you're there. Your doctor prescribes *Tamiflu*.

Costs under Part B

Since you have already met the Part B Deductible for the year, you pay the 20% co-insurance on the Medicare-approved charges, which are:

- Office visit, approved amount - $83.08, you pay 20% = $16.62
- Nasal swab, approved amount - $20.69, you pay 20% = $4.14
- Chest x-ray, approved amount - $36.86, you pay 20% = $7.37

Your total out of pocket costs are $28.13 for the office visits and tests. We haven't talked very much about drugs yet, so this is a good time to make sure you know that Original Medicare, Parts A and B, don't cover prescription drugs (except in extraordinary circumstances, which we will cover in the next section). This means you will pay full retail price for your Tamiflu, (about $155).

IMPORTANT NOTE: I am not a physician or medical biller, so the amounts I used should only be considered estimates; in some cases they are based on actual billing codes, but for past years, (2017-2020). Also, the example visits, treatments, and tests may not reflect the most likely treatment prescribed by a doctor. The main point is the estimate of out of pocket costs, which are shown to give you an idea of what these services might cost. The amounts shown should not be considered official.

Example #2 – You fall while jogging and wrench your back and hip. You go to the doctor and receive an x-ray, MRI, and are prescribed five physical therapy visits.

Costs under Part B

You have already met your deductible for the year, so you pay the 20% co-insurance on the Medicare-approved charges, which are:

- Office visit, approved amount - $83.08, you pay 20% = $16.62
- Back x-ray, approved amount - $44.03, you pay 20% = $8.81
- MRI, approved amount - $305, you pay 20% = $61
- Physical therapy evaluation – approved amount - $110, you pay 20% = $22
- Physical therapy sessions, 4 days, approved amount - $93 x 4, you pay 20% = $74.40

Example #3 – You are diagnosed with lung cancer, and you receive intravenous chemotherapy treatment for six months.

Costs under Part B

You have already met the deductible, so you pay 20% of the Medicare-approved charges. Finding accurate information on chemotherapy costs is difficult, but at an average cost of $6,000 per month for six months, total charges are $36,000. You pay 20%, or $7,200. Note that this is just for the chemotherapy; it doesn't include the cost of testing, biopsy, doctor's visits and oncologists. If you are hospitalized as an inpatient, you also pay the Part A Deductible. Cancer is obviously a serious and expensive disease, and your costs under Medicare can be quite high.

Remember this key point: there is no limit on your out of pocket spending with Original Medicare. If your chemo is more expensive, lasts longer, or if you have three different hospital stays in three separate benefit periods, you are going to rack up some high out of pocket costs. *You will never hit a yearly or lifetime maximum.*

Also remember that prescription drugs are not covered by Original Medicare. You will be out of pocket for all your prescription drug costs unless you choose a private Medicare Part D prescription drug plan (see next chapter).

QUESTION #6 – Didn't you say there were a few drugs Medicare will cover?

ANSWER #6 – Yes, there are some medications covered by Part B. Some of them are cancer drugs, like oral chemotherapy treatments. Besides these, Part B generally covers medications you don't normally give yourself, for example:

- Injectable osteoporosis drugs
- Other injectable and infused drugs
- Organ transplant drugs

The details matter here, like whether or not an oral drug is also available in an injectable form. For planning purposes, I recommend you assume you'll get no drug coverage from Part B.

What To Remember:

- You will pay out of pocket for most services with Medicare
- Your costs are not capped each year in Original Medicare
- Most drugs are not covered by Original Medicare

Chapter 3 – Part D Prescription Drug Plans

M

To be perfectly honest, I don't know why Medicare wasn't designed to help people with prescription drug coverage. Maybe it was because medications didn't cost as much in the '60s, or maybe it was simply an oversight. Either way, prescriptions weren't covered by Medicare for a long time. But as the cost of medications rose over time, and as the number of drugs prescribed grew also, the burden of paying for them increased. Eventually, in 2003, Congress and then-*President Bush* enacted legislation that provided an option for drug coverage for Medicare beneficiaries. Thus, Part D of Medicare was born.

Medicare Part D plans are offered by private insurance companies and are designed to help you pay for, and save money on, your medication. The key to remember here is that you're going to be expected to pay for part of every prescription you fill unless your plan offers a deal like $0 copayment on generic drugs or something similar.

The enactment of Part D provided two ways to receive prescription drug coverage for Medicare beneficiaries:

- Standalone Prescription Drug Plans (PDPs), or from
- Medicare Advantage Prescription Drug Plans (MAPDs)

Under the rules of Part D, Medicare Supplement Plans are no longer allowed to offer drug coverage to new policyholders.

We will return to the types of plans you can use, but for now I would like to mention Medicare Supplement (Medigap) drug coverage. Before 2006, some Medigap plans (H, I, and J) did offer drug coverage, but these plans are not available to new members or policyholders after 12/31/2005. People did have the option to keep their existing coverage, and some did. However, many dropped these plans and instead enrolled in the two new types of drug plan.

All Part D plans work in basically the same way, whether you have a standalone PDP, or an MAPD plan. However, you cannot combine them. For instance, if you choose a regular Medicare Advantage Plan, without prescription drug coverage, you can't add a standalone PDP to it (with one exception that will probably not be relevant for most people). If you want drug coverage with a Medicare Advantage Plan, you must choose an MAPD.

On the other hand, you can choose to stay in Original Medicare, add a Medicare Supplement Plan, and also enroll in a standalone PDP. In fact many people choose to do just that. So, here's a quick review of your drug plan options at this point:

- Choose a Medicare Advantage Plan with drug coverage (MAPD),
  or
- Stay with Original Medicare and choose a standalone Prescription Drug Plan (PDP). You could also add Medicare Supplement (Medigap) if you'd like to.

We will go into all the details on Medicare Advantage and Medicare Supplement Insurance later on, but I wanted to make sure your overall options are clear from the beginning.

Back to prescription drug coverage, regardless of which option you choose. As you're familiar with by now, these plans don't cover 100% of your costs. You will have a range of out of pocket costs, including:

- Monthly premiums
- Annual deductible
- Per-prescription co-payments and co-insurance
- There is no cap on your total drug spending under Part D

Monthly premiums for Part D plans vary. If you use a Medicare Advantage Plan, you might not have any monthly premium. For 2021, the national average monthly premium for standalone Prescription Drug Plans is $41 (Cubanski & Damico, 2020). That's an average; some are more and others less per month.

The same goes for a deductible; many plans don't have an annual deductible, but others do. The maximum permissible deductible for 2021 is $445. You might have to pay up to this amount in a year before your drug plan will begin helping you pay for your medication. Here is an insider tip though—many Part D plans will waive the deductible on Tier 1 and Tier 2 medication (more on Tiers later, but just know for now that these are generic or otherwise inexpensive drugs). If you only take generic medication, you may not have to pay the deductible at all.

This is a good time to talk about coverage stages. Your co-payments or co-coinsurance amounts (once you've paid the deductible, if any) will change throughout the calendar year as you and your insurance company pay for medication. The amounts you pay change based on your movement through four Coverage Stages. We've already discussed the first Coverage Stage: the deductible stage. Here's a quick summary of all four:

- Coverage Stage 1 – Deductible stage – You pay full price until you have met the deductible (up to $445 for 2021)
- Coverage Stage 2 – Initial Coverage stage – During this stage, you will pay your plan's co-insurance or co-payment for every filled prescription. You will keep paying your standard co-pays/co-insurance until your total drug costs (what you *and* your insurance company have paid together) for the year hit $4,130
- Coverage Stage 3 – Coverage Gap – Once your total drug costs hit $4,130, you will pay 25% of the cost for both generic and brand name drugs. You will pay this co-insurance amount until your personal drug costs (just you, *excluding* your insurance company, unlike the calculation for Coverage Stage 2) hit $6,550, then you move to the next stage
- Coverage Stage 4 – Catastrophic Coverage – In this stage, you will pay a small co-pay, or 5% of the total cost of your medication, whichever is higher. You stay in this stage until January 1st of the next year

As you can see, your costs will vary depending on how many prescriptions you fill, and what kinds of medication you use. No one wants to spend thousands of dollars a year for prescriptions, but there is some good news for those who hit Stage 3 / the Coverage Gap. To run the calculation for your total personal drug costs (known as TrOOP – True Out Of Pocket costs), you get to add in the value of drug maker discounts. This is very helpful, because the drug companies are required by law to discount the price of their medication by 70% for people in the Coverage Gap. Here is a breakdown of the costs in this stage for brand name drugs:

- Drug company provides a 70% discount off the full retail price
- You pay 25% of the full retail price
- Your plan pays the remaining 5% of the full retail price

You get to add your costs (25%) *and* the drug maker discount (70%) when calculating your total drug costs. This will get you out of Stage 3 and into Stage 4 much quicker than if you only count your actual, out of pocket spending.

For generic drugs, the costs are broken down like this:

- Medicare pays 75% of the full retail cost of your generic medication
- You pay the remaining 25% of the full retail cost for generics

Some plans may provide bonus coverage in the Coverage Gap, but they aren't required to, and most do not.

QUESTION # 1 – What counts as my out of pocket costs?

ANSWER #1 – Basically any amounts you pay for medication count. Amounts you pay for coverage, like premiums, do not count as drug costs. Also, any prescriptions you have filled that aren't covered by your plan's formulary (more on plan formularies shortly) do not count towards this total. This makes it critically important to use medication that your plan covers, especially if you are likely to get anywhere near the Coverage Gap stage.

Formularies And Tiers

You need to know that Part D drug plans are not required to cover every medication available. Instead, each plan has its own Formulary. The Formulary is a list of every medication and vaccine the plan covers. Anything not specifically stated in the Formulary is not covered by the plan. If you fill a prescription for a non-covered drug, you will pay full retail price for it.

However, there are certain categories of medication for which plans are required to cover all, or substantially all available drugs. These categories include:

- Antiretrovirals
- Immunosuppressants
- Anticancer drugs
- Antidepressants

- Anticonvulsants
- Antipsychotics

Besides these six protected categories, all Part D plans must cover at least two medications in every 'therapeutic category'. A therapeutic category is a group of medications that help with a common condition. For instance, cholesterol medications or thyroid medicines. The key thing is to know that every plan must have at least two thyroid medications (for example), but they are not required to cover *every* thyroid drug on the market.

Each plan decides which mix of drugs it will cover. Because of this, you should always check the drug plan Formulary to make sure all medication you take will be covered. I check this for my clients. *If you downloaded your Mastering Medicare Handbook, there is a place for you to write them all down.* Having all your medication and doses summarized in one place makes checking plan formularies much easier.

Within each plan's formulary, the medications are grouped into different 'Tiers'. A Tier, as we briefly mentioned before, is a pricing level. A Part D plan may have up to five tiers, but it's more common to see four. The four most commons tiers are:

- Tier 1 – preferred generic drugs
- Tier 2 – non-preferred generics and preferred brand name drugs
- Tier 3 – non-preferred brand name drugs
- Tier 4 – specialty drugs

Your cost sharing (co-pay or co-insurance amount) varies by Tier. The higher the Tier, the higher your out of pocket costs.

You can see that the amount you'll pay for medication is fluid. Each medication you take could be in a different Tier. You will pay different costs for each Tier. In addition, as you move from one Coverage Stage to another, your cost sharing changes, even for the same drugs you've been taking all along.

This can be very confusing, so here's a quick example. I won't use any drug names, or Part D plan names to 'protect the innocent', but you should be able to get the gist from this example.

You take a total of five medications:

- A name brand insulin, Tier 3, full retail price $485
- A name brand arthritis medication, Tier 4, full retail price $3,625
- A generic diabetes drug, Tier 1, full retail price $19
- A generic cholesterol medication, Tier 1 full retail price $13
- A name brand opioid for chronic back pain, Tier 3, full retail price $225

Your plan has the following cost structure by coverage stage:

- Coverage Stage 1 - $445 deductible
- Coverage Stage 2 - $3 co-pay for Tier 1, $7 co-pay for Tier 2, $33 co-pay for Tier 3, and $133 co-pay for Tier 4
- Coverage Stage 3 – 25% of full retail price for brand name and 25% of full retail price for generic medication

- Coverage Stage 4 – No more than 5% of full retail price

Your plan has a deductible, but you hit it the very first month of the year, due to the price of your opioid and arthritis medication. You pay:

- $445 in full price, and
- $205 in co-payments

Your total out of pocket costs in January are $650. However, your total drug costs (used to determine when you move from Coverage Stage 2 to Coverage Stage 3) are much higher—they are based on the full retail price of your drugs. After just one month, your total drug costs are $4,367 (the total retail cost of one month's supply of your medication).

In February, you fill the same prescriptions. However, because of the cost of your most expensive drug (the Tier 4 arthritis medication), you move into the Coverage Gap. You will pay 25% of the retail cost of your medicines until you move into the Catastrophic Coverage stage.

I can't break out the per-prescription cost for February because timing matters here: you might pay a regular co-payment before you move into the Coverage Gap, it's impossible to say. Your out of pocket costs would likely be between $205 (total of co-pays under Coverage Stage 1) and $1,092 (what you pay at 25% of drug cost in the Coverage Gap [Stage 3]). For the sake of our illustration, we will assume you pay $918. We will also assume that the value of the manufacturer discount you received in the Coverage Gap for February was $1,043.

To be clear, I can't provide you with a specific amount here because the *order in which your prescriptions are filled* will dictate when your total drug costs move you into the Coverage Gap.

For March, your total retail drug costs are $4,367. You will pay 25% of this (regardless of name brand or generic), or $1,092. Remember your drug manufacturer discounts get added to your 'total drug costs', so your total for this month is actually $3,784 ($1,092 you actually paid, plus 70% of the cost of your name brand drugs. In this case, 70% x $4,335, or $3,035). Now, your total out of pocket drug costs plus manufacturer's discounts has come to $6,738 for the year. You have moved to Catastrophic Coverage (Stage 4). For the rest of the year, you will pay no more than 5% of total retail cost for your medication.

For April through the end of December, your maximum out of pocket cost is $218.35 per month (5% of $4,367). I should point out here, there is no cap on your annual drug spending, unlike the cap on your health care spending with Medicare Advantage (chapter 5) or some Medicare Supplement Insurance plans (chapter 4).

For the full year, you paid $4,625, which is obviously a large amount of money. However, if you had paid full retail price for these prescriptions, you would have paid $52,404 ($4,367 full retail price x 12 months).

As you can see, these calculations can be complicated. It gets even more complicated if you're prescribed a new medication in the middle of the year.

Hopefully you can see though, that your Part D drug plan can save you some serious money.

One more thing to keep in mind is that your total out of pocket drug costs are only calculated on medications covered by your plan. So, if you pay out of pocket for a non-covered medication, it won't count towards your total drug spending, which will delay getting to the Catastrophic Coverage Stage. Do *not* do this—only use a drug plan that will cover the medication you take.

QUESTION # 2 – What if I need a drug that's not on my plan's Formulary?

ANSWER #2 –First of all, if it's a medication you currently take, make sure that any Part D plan (whether Medicare Advantage or standalone PDP) covers the medication before you enroll in it. You can check the plan's website, or call the plan directly to find out. If you are working with an independent insurance agent, they should be willing to do this for you.

On the other hand, what if something changes with your health in the middle of the year, after you're already enrolled in a Part D plan, and a new prescription is not on your plan's formulary? Are you condemned to paying full price out of your own pocket? No, you have some options. You can ask for a Formulary Exception from your Part D plan. In this case, you would ask them to cover a drug that isn't on their formulary. You will likely need to have your doctor complete the Formulary Exception request; they will have to indicate why you must have the non-covered drug. Your plan is not required to approve Formulary Exception requests, but they often do, and are required to consider them. You may be required to try other, covered medication before your plan will cover the new medication.

QUESTION # 3 – Are there any other restrictions on medication, other than the Formulary?

ANSWER #3 – Yes, there are some other restrictions you may encounter with Part D drug plans. You might encounter:

- Quantity limits (the amount of medication is limited);
- Step therapy (a requirement to try less potent or lower cost medication before more expensive or stronger medication. You are likely to encounter this with medications like opiates, which have strong side-effects or other dangers).

What To Remember:

- You can get Part D coverage from either a standalone PDP or an MAPD
- Every Part D drug plan has a Formulary, or list of covered drugs—make sure your drugs are covered before enrolling in any plan
- Your costs for medication can change throughout the year as you move through the four Coverage Stages
- There is no cap on your drug spending during the year

Chapter 4 – Medicare Supplement Insurance

M

By now you should have a good grasp on what Medicare is and how it works. You probably feel like it's pretty good coverage, but you might have more out of pocket costs than you would prefer. And it's true: Medicare *does* provide comprehensive benefits for a *good* price. After all, have you seen the cost of individual, private insurance for people in their 60's? It is *not* cheap! On the other hand, those out of pocket costs can add up. And, if you should have the misfortune to have major health events like multiple hospitalizations, lengthy hospital stays, or cancer treatments under Part B, you could see those out of pocket costs grow to tens of thousands of dollars. To help reduce or eliminate some of these costs, many of my clients use Medicare Supplement Insurance. Medicare Supplement is also frequently called Medigap because it is designed to fill in some of the 'gaps' in Original Medicare—those costs that you're expected to pay.

Medicare Supplement Insurance has been around as long as Medicare itself. Medigap coverage is provided by private health insurance companies and is specifically designed to work with Original Medicare. Your Original Medicare coverage through Parts A and B functions as your primary coverage, and pays the majority of your benefits. Medicare Supplement pays for part of the rest of your expenses. For this reason, when you go to the doctor or other provider, you will have to bring both your Medicare card and your Medicare Supplement Insurance card with you.

The benefits provided by Medicare Supplement Insurance plans are regulated by federal and state laws. These laws mandate that Medigap plans offer standardized benefits. This means that the coverage provided by any specific Medigap plan is the same, regardless of where you live, and which insurance company you choose. These plans are standardized across forty-seven of the fifty states. Wisconsin, Minnesota, and Massachusetts have their own, individual, Medicare Supplement laws. For the rest of our meeting, we'll talk about the plans available in the standardized states.

There are ten standardized Medicare Supplement Insurance plans, and they are identified by letter: Plans A, B, C, D, F, G, K, L, M, and N. There are 'high deductible' versions of Plans F and G. Medigap Plans C, F, and High Deductible F are not available for anyone who becomes eligible for Medicare on or after January 1st, 2020. If you were eligible before that date, even if you didn't enter Medicare because you were still working, you have a protected right to enroll in those plans. You are 'grandfathered in' as we say.

Each one of the standardized plans covers a slightly different portion of the gaps in Original Medicare. Before we dive in to the details of what each plan covers, remember these are all standardized. So, Medigap Plan A from *Aetna* provides the exact same core benefits as Plan A from *United Healthcare*, and these benefits are the same in all forty-seven of the standardized states. We'll talk more about how the insurance companies differ in a little bit, but for now, let's dive in to what each of the standardized plans covers.

Medigap Plan A

This is the most basic plan, sort of an introductory Medigap plan. Plan A covers these gaps:

- Part A co-insurance hospital costs for up to 365 additional days beyond Original Medicare
- Part B co-insurance (it pays your 20% share, completely)
- Your first three pints of blood (Original Medicare covers anything beyond this)
- Part A hospice care co-insurance / co-payment

And that's it. Plan A does not provide any coverage for:

- Part A co-insurance for Skilled Nursing Care
- Part A deductible
- Part B deductible
- Part B excess charges
- Foreign travel emergency coverage

Medigap Plan B

Plan B is slightly more comprehensive than Plan A. It covers the same elements, as well as the Part A deductible. Plan B covers:

- Part A co-insurance hospital costs for up to 365 additional days beyond Original Medicare
- Part B co-insurance (it pays your 20% share, completely)
- Your first three pints of blood (Original Medicare covers anything beyond this)

- Part A hospice care co-insurance / co-payment
- Part A deductible

Plan B leaves these gaps un-covered:

- Part A co-insurance for Skilled Nursing Care
- Part B deductible
- Part B excess charges
- Foreign travel emergency coverage

Medigap Plan C

This is a pretty comprehensive plan. Plan C covers:

- Part A co-insurance hospital costs for up to 365 additional days beyond Original Medicare
- Part B co-insurance (it pays your 20% share, completely)
- Your first three pints of blood (Original Medicare covers anything beyond this)
- Part A hospice care co-insurance / co-payment
- Part A deductible
- Part A co-insurance for Skilled Nursing Care
- Part B deductible
- Foreign travel emergency coverage (up to 80%)

There is only one gap that Plan C doesn't cover—Part B excess charges. You may never experience these though if you use providers who accept Medicare Assignment. So with Plan C, you might not have any out of pocket costs for medical expenses.

Medigap Plan D

Plan D is almost as comprehensive as Plan C. The only difference is Plan D doesn't cover the Part B deductible. Plan D covers:

- Part A co-insurance hospital costs for up to 365 additional days beyond Original Medicare
- Part B co-insurance (it pays your 20% share, completely)
- Your first three pints of blood (Original Medicare covers anything beyond this)
- Part A hospice care co-insurance / co-payment
- Part A deductible
- Part A co-insurance for Skilled Nursing Care
- Foreign travel emergency coverage (up to 80%)

The only items Plan D does not cover for you are:

- Part B deductible
- Part B excess charges

Medigap Plan F

For years Plan F was the gold standard of Medigap coverage. It closes every gap in original Medicare. For this reason it was often referred to as 'Plan Fabulous'. I just said it covered everything, but here's what that looks like in bullet-point form:

- Part A co-insurance hospital costs for up to 365 additional days beyond Original Medicare
- Part B co-insurance (it pays your 20% share, completely)
- Your first three pints of blood (Original Medicare covers anything beyond this)
- Part A hospice care co-insurance / co-payment
- Part A deductible

- Part A co-insurance for Skilled Nursing Care
- Part B deductible
- Part B excess charges
- Foreign travel emergency coverage (up to 80%)

Medigap Plan G

Plan G has replaced Plans C and F as the most comprehensive plan for people new to Medicare on or after January 1st, 2020. This plan covers all of your out of pocket costs except for the Part B deductible:

- Part A co-insurance hospital costs for up to 365 additional days beyond Original Medicare
- Part B co-insurance (it pays your 20% share, completely)
- Your first three pints of blood (Original Medicare covers anything beyond this)
- Part A hospice care co-insurance / co-payment
- Part A deductible
- Part A co-insurance for Skilled Nursing Care
- Part B excess charges
- Foreign travel emergency coverage (up to 80%)

With Plan G, you will pay no more than $203 out of pocket for Medicare-approved expenses (2021 Part B deductible). All other gaps are covered at 100% (except for international travel, which is covered at 80%).

Medigap Plan K

Plan K offers partial coverage of most of the gaps in Original Medicare:

- 100% coverage of Part A co-insurance hospital costs for up to 365 additional days beyond Original Medicare
- 50% of Part B co-insurance (it pays half of your 20% share)
- 50% of the cost for your first three pints of blood (Original Medicare covers anything beyond this)
- 50% coverage of Part A hospice care co-insurance / co-payment
- 50% coverage of Part A deductible
- 50% coverage of Part A co-insurance for Skilled Nursing Care
- Out of pocket limit of $6,220 for 2021

Plan K offers no coverage of:

- Part B deductible
- Part B excess charges
- Foreign travel emergency coverage

Medigap Plan L

Plan L is very similar to Plan K, with coverage of:

- 100% coverage of Part A co-insurance hospital costs for up to 365 additional days beyond Original Medicare
- 75% of Part B co-insurance (it pays ¾ of your 20% share)
- 75% of the cost for your first three pints of blood (Original Medicare covers anything beyond this)
- 75% coverage of Part A hospice care co-insurance / co-payment

- 75% coverage of Part A deductible
- 75% coverage of Part A co-insurance for Skilled Nursing Care
- Out of pocket limit of $3,110 for 2021

Just like Plan K, Plan L offers no coverage for:

- Part B deductible
- Part B excess charges
- Foreign travel emergency coverage

Medigap Plan M

Plan M is sort of a hybrid of Plans K/L and D, with coverage for:

- Part A co-insurance hospital costs for up to 365 additional days beyond Original Medicare
- Part B co-insurance (it pays your 20% share, completely)
- Your first three pints of blood (Original Medicare covers anything beyond this)
- Part A hospice care co-insurance / co-payment
- 50% of Part A deductible
- Part A co-insurance for Skilled Nursing Care
- Foreign travel emergency coverage (up to 80%)

Plan M provides no coverage for:

- Part B deductible
- Part B excess charges

Medigap Plan N

Plan N is a comprehensive plan with a feature that makes it resemble traditional employer or individual health insurance. Plan N covers:

- Part A co-insurance hospital costs for up to 365 additional days beyond Original Medicare
- 100% of your Part B co-insurance, except that you will pay a $20 co-pay for office visits and $50 co-pay for emergency room visits (waived if you're admitted as an inpatient)
- Your first three pints of blood (Original Medicare covers anything beyond this)
- Part A hospice care co-insurance / co-payment
- 100% of Part A deductible
- Part A co-insurance for Skilled Nursing Care
- Foreign travel emergency coverage (up to 80%)

Plan N does not cover Part B excess charges or the Part B deductible.

So there you have all the options available to you for Medigap coverage. Remember, the coverage details will be the same for every single insurance company. This is a huge help in determining what your coverage should be. How? Because you can focus on choosing the *benefits* you need first and foremost. Don't worry about choosing the specific insurance company. First, make a decision on how much coverage you need.

Here is a real-world example. My clients, we'll call them Mr. and Mrs. C, have a number of serious health conditions. They have been hospitalized in the past, take several medications, and are worried about high out-of-pocket spending. For this reason, they selected Medigap Plan G. They wanted to know, for sure, that they wouldn't have to pay tens of thousands of dollars if they had hospital stays or other health issues.

On the other hand, you may have good health, and come from a family who has a good health history. You are not worried about your health, but you really like the idea of being able to see any doctor in the country, without network or referral restrictions (more on this later). You might be better off enrolling in Plan N or B. You don't need the most comprehensive plan around, you just want to have most of your gaps covered, and maximum physician flexibility. Make these decisions first, and then look for the insurance company that's right for you. How will you know? That's what we'll talk about now!

What Differentiates Medicare Supplement Insurance Companies?

We have already said the basic benefits are identical from company to company. However, there are differences in three areas:

- Price / premiums
- Extra benefits
- Stability / reputation

Since these are supplemental health insurance policies, each insurance company sets its own premiums. There is competition between them though, so their premiums tend to be similar to one another. Companies can set their rates in various ways (by age at issue, age at renewal, or for the community as a whole). Some states restrict how insurance companies set and change their rates. There is no real need to dive into the details here, just understand that any outlier (very low premium compared to its peers) will probably lead to higher-than-normal rate increases in the future. Large, stable companies tend to increase their premiums by 2.5% to 4.5% per year.

Once you've chosen the level of coverage you want, find the company with the lowest, sustainable and stable premium possible, taking into account your need for extra benefits.

Extra benefits are just what they sound like: benefits beyond the standard. Every company has the right to offer extras, or not; it's up to them. Extra benefits for Medigap plans often take the form of:

- Vision discounts (on exams, lenses and frames)
- Health and fitness memberships
- Hearing and prescription drug discounts
- Access to 24/7 nurse hotlines

Notice that these are not *coverages*, they're discounts. You will pay less than full price, but it's not like you're getting comprehensive coverage. However, these discounts can be valuable, especially if you're inclined to use the gym or need glasses. Of course nothing is truly free, so Medigap plans with many extra benefits likely have higher premiums. This isn't a problem as long as you make an informed decision. Again, start with your basic coverage needs, review premium cost, and then look at what, if any, extra benefits come with your coverage. If you don't care about extra benefits, just go with the cheapest reputable carrier.

The reputation, or stability, of an insurance company can be broken-down into two broad categories:

- Financial strength and maturity in the market
- Customer service

Let's take customer service first. Honestly, I tell all of my clients not to dwell on this too much. I mean... they're insurance companies! Nobody loves dealing with insurance companies. Plus, people have a tendency to leave negative reviews over positive ones, so take any kind of online rating with a 'grain of salt'. On the other hand, if you have a particular 'bone to pick' with a company, you should be able to find a different one as there is a lot of competition in this market.

An under-appreciated point is to make sure the company you use has been in the Medicare Supplement Insurance market for a while; preferably ten or more years. Also, check their financial strength rating. These are frequently provided by *Moody's*, *A.M. Best*, and *S&P*. This information can be complicated and hard to find, so I strongly encourage you to work with an independent health insurance agent as they can give you all the details you need. And, if they are truly independent, they have no incentive to steer you into any particular Medigap plan or provider.

QUESTION # 1 – Medigap sounds good to me. When do I sign up?

ANSWER #1 – There are two main types of enrollment into Medicare Supplement Insurance. The first type is called Guaranteed Issue, and the second is Medically Underwritten.

Of the two types, Guaranteed Issue is much better and easier to understand and use. This is exactly what it sounds like—you apply for coverage, and your coverage is guaranteed to be issued. To be more specific, this means:

- An insurance company must issue you the policy you apply for, and
- You can't be charged a higher premium based on your current or prior health status

You can qualify for Guaranteed Issue in two different ways. The first way to get Medigap coverage under Guaranteed Issue terms is during your Medigap Open Enrollment Period. Everyone who becomes eligible for Medicare will have a Medigap Open Enrollment Period. This is a six-month enrollment window during which you can sign up for any Medigap plan available in your state. The Medigap Open Enrollment Period begins when *both* of these statements are true:

- You are 65 years old, or older, and
- You are enrolled in Medicare Part B

Pay attention to these criteria because they are important. Your Medigap Open Enrollment Period doesn't start until you actually enter Part B. This doesn't always happen at age 65, which is where this can get tricky. For instance, if you work past age 65 and delay taking Part B until you're 69 or 70, that's when your Open Enrollment Period will begin. You will not 'miss' your Medigap Open Enrollment Period just because you delayed taking Part B past age 65. On the other hand, if you enter Medicare Part B *before* you turn 65, due to disability or illness, your Medigap Open Enrollment Period will not start *until you actually turn 65*. As an extreme example, I have helped people with Medicare who were in their twenties. They will have to wait about forty years, but eventually they will enter their Medigap Open Enrollment Period—once they turn 65.

The best time to enroll in Medicare Supplement Insurance is during your Open Enrollment Period. You won't have to answer health questions; you cannot be turned down. You won't pay a higher premium due to your health, nor will you be subject to any kind of pre-existing condition restrictions.

QUESTION # 2 – Are there other ways to qualify for Guaranteed Issue?

ANSWER #2 – Yes, but they depend on your circumstances. Many people will not qualify for a second Guaranteed Issue period, but it is possible. Here are the most common ways to qualify for an additional Guaranteed Issue period:

- You move to a new county or state, and that move gives you new Medicare Insurance plan options
- You chose Medicare Advantage when you first entered Medicare at age 65, and have been in the plan for less than twelve months
- You dropped Medicare Supplement coverage for your first Medicare Advantage plan

(regardless of age), and you've been on it for less than twelve months
- Your Medicare Advantage plan loses its contract with CMS, or fails to renew it

There are some other reasons, having to do with your Medigap company going bankrupt, or losing employer coverage, but these are fairly rare.

Unless you choose Medigap during your initial Open Enrollment Period, or you qualify for one of the other Guaranteed Issue periods, you will have to undergo Medical Underwriting. This can sound kind of scary and insurance agents sometimes make it sound even worse. But for many people, Medical Underwriting will not prevent you from getting Medigap coverage. So, what is Medical Underwriting?

Medical Underwriting means that when you apply for coverage, you answer health-related questions, and the insurance company can investigate your health history (pharmacy check and a report from the Medical Information Bureau). Your answers and the results of the pharmacy and Medical Information Bureau check can lead to one of three results:
- Policy issued at preferred rates
- Policy issued at non-preferred (higher) rates
- Coverage declined, no policy issued

You can also be subject to waiting periods for pre-existing conditions discovered during your underwriting. For example, if it's discovered that your doctor recommends you get back surgery, the insurer may impose a waiting period on this procedure before they will cover it.

You can see that because of these restrictions, it is far better to enroll in Medigap during your Open Enrollment Period. If you don't take advantage at that time, you can't be certain you'll be able to qualify for the coverage at a later time should you want it then.

QUESTION # 3 – What about drug coverage? Can I get that with Medicare Supplement Insurance?

ANSWER #3 – We touched on this briefly before, but to be plain here, no, you can't get drug coverage from Medigap policies. If you want Medicare Supplement Insurance, you'll have to enroll in a standalone Part D drug plan to get drug coverage.

QUESTION # 4 – Are there any network or referral restrictions?

ANSWER #4 – No, not at all. This is perhaps the most popular benefit of Medicare Supplement Insurance. You retain total freedom to see any doctor in the nation who accepts Medicare patients. This feature really appeals to people who want the ability to travel, even out of state if necessary, to see the 'best' specialist for various conditions.

Real World Case Study

Mr. C was retiring at the end of 2017 and would be losing his employer health insurance. His wife, Mrs. C, would also be losing her health coverage. They would enter Medicare on January 1, 2018.

Mr. and Mrs. C had a history of multiple chronic illnesses. Combined, they took quite a few medications. They were concerned about paying high out of pocket medical expenses. Co-payments here and there for doctor's appointments didn't bother them, but what kept them up at night, so to speak, was having a major illness and hospitalization that would require them to pay thousands of dollars out of pocket.

We reviewed their options for Medicare Advantage and Medicare Supplement Insurance. After considering their health history and the coverage available, they elected to stick with Original Medicare and purchase Medicare Supplement Insurance Plan G for each of them. They also enrolled in separate Prescription Drug Plans.

In essence, they decided that they would rather pay a *known* premium amount each month than face *unknown* out of pocket costs due to a medical emergency. Since they were relocating to a more rural area, they also wanted the ability to see any doctor that accepted Medicare patients without network restrictions or referral requirements.

They enrolled in their plans in November of 2017. Their Medicare Supplement and Prescription Drug coverage took effect on 1/1/2018. On January 3rd, two days after their coverage began, Mr. C went to the hospital with severe heart symptoms. He was admitted to the hospital and ended up having emergency heart surgery. He remained hospitalized for several days.

His total costs for his hospital stay, surgery, and all medical treatment due to the illness was $183. In fact, that's all he paid for all of his Medicare-approved health care, including follow-up appointments, for the entire year. That is the power of Medicare Supplement Insurance.

It should be said that he did have costs relating to prescription drugs, and that due to the types and amounts of medications taken, his drug costs were significantly more than the $183 he paid for his Part B deductible (2018 amount). However, he would have paid those drug costs regardless of whether he chose Medicare Supplement or Medicare Advantage.

What To Remember:

- The best time to enroll in Medigap is during your six month Open Enrollment Period
- You will need to get a standalone Prescription Drug Plan if you choose Medigap
- Base benefits for all ten Medigap plans are *standardized* across every insurance company in forty-seven states
- Medicare Supplement plans offer maximum access to physicians, without referral requirements

Chapter 5 – Part C – Medicare Advantage Plans

M

Medicare Advantage plans are your other option for protecting yourself against high out of pocket expenses in Medicare. These plans work a little differently than Original Medicare plus Medigap. Medicare Advantage is also known as Part C, and these plans are an alternative way to receive your Medicare Part A and B benefits through a private insurance company.

When I say it's an 'alternative', I mean just that—when you enroll in a Medicare Advantage plan, you actually disenroll from Original Medicare. Now that kind of scares people sometimes, but you shouldn't let it scare you. A Medicare Advantage plan must cover everything that Original Medicare covers. This is literally mandated in a contract between the insurance company and Centers for Medicare and Medicaid Services, (CMS—the government entity that administers the Medicare program). The Medicare Advantage program is highly regulated, and CMS is quick to enforce the rules when needed. So you can be confident that if Original Medicare covers something, a Medicare Advantage plan will too. Note, there is technically one exception to this—hospice benefits. However, even if you are in Medicare Advantage, you still get hospice benefits from Part A, so you are covered in that direction either way.

Medicare Advantage plans are not really about the minimum legal requirements though. All Medicare Advantage plans have a standard feature that makes them stand out from Original Medicare—*all* Medicare Advantage plans have an Annual Out Of Pocket Maximum (OOPM) limit. In other words, Part C plans give you the peace of mind that no matter what happens with your health, your costs will be capped. This is the first major difference between Original Medicare and Part C plans. There are some others too.

Medicare Advantage plans often offer more benefits than Original Medicare. These are called Extra Benefits. These kinds of benefits are not available under either Part A or B. Extra Benefits can include:

- Vision coverage (vision exams, lenses, and sometimes frames)
- Hearing coverage (hearing exams, and sometimes reduced price hearing aids)
- Dental (either integrated within the plan or available for a low additional premium)
- Transportation to and from medical appointments
- Fitness / gym memberships (free access to gyms and/or online fitness programs)
- Over-the-counter products (monthly or quarterly credit towards the purchase of non-prescription medical supplies)
- Safety monitoring equipment and services
- Worldwide emergency coverage

QUESTION # 1 – Do all Medicare Advantage Plans offer these benefits?

ANSWER #1 – No, not all Part C plans offer these, but most do. Also, not every plan will offer every possible Extra Benefit, but most plans do offer some. The most popular are vision and hearing benefits. Insurance companies offer these extras for a variety of reasons, including:

- To attract new members
- To retain existing members
- To improve the overall health and wellness of the people they are insuring

And yes, insurance companies aren't offering these Extra Benefits just to make life better for you. They hope that more members in better health will lead to more profits. However, in this case, I think their interests are aligned with yours—you need vision, hearing, or dental coverage, your insurance company wants more members, you want to be active, healthy, and vital, your insurance company wants to pay fewer claims related to chronic illnesses. You might as well make the most of these benefits; use them to your advantage (pun sort of intended).

Another big difference between Medicare Advantage and Original Medicare relates to prescription drug coverage. Original Medicare only covers prescription medications in very limited circumstances. However, many Medicare Advantage Plans provide drug coverage that meets the Part D requirements. This means you can combine your hospital, medical, and drug benefits in one plan. This is even more useful when you realize you won't pay a separate premium for your drug coverage. We'll talk about Medicare Advantage pricing in just a bit, but for now just understand that MAPD's (Medicare Advantage Plans with Part D drug coverage) have a single premium and provide creditable drug coverage.

QUESTION #2 – What if I don't like the drug benefit of my Medicare Advantage Plan? Can I add a standalone Prescription Drug Plan?

ANSWER #2 – Unfortunately, probably not. Except in very limited cases, you can't have Medicare Advantage and standalone drug coverage. The exception is for what's called a Private Fee For Service (PFFS) Medicare Advantage plan, and even then, only if that plan doesn't offer drug coverage. These are fairly unpopular Part C plans, and they are not nearly as available as HMO or PPO plans. Most people I work with for Medicare don't have access to these plans, so we'll ignore them. If you need drug coverage and want Medicare Advantage, make sure you choose a plan that incorporates drug coverage.

How Does Medicare Advantage Work?

These plans work just like any private, individual or employer-provided health insurance you've had in the last twenty years. Most Medicare Advantage plans fall into one of two types:

- Health Maintenance Organizations (HMO), or
- Preferred Provider Organizations (PPO)

As we touched on a moment ago, there are a couple of obscure Medicare Advantage plan types, but we're not going to cover them because they're rarely available and rarely chosen. If you have a real hankering to learn about these rare types, you can find more information on medicare.gov.

HMOs are definitely the most common and most popular. As you likely know, HMOs work within the framework of networks of providers. A Medicare Advantage HMO contracts with providers like doctors, laboratories, and hospitals. You must generally use network providers in order to have your services and procedures covered. This cannot be overstated – do *not* go out of network with an HMO unless your plan has authorized such an action. You will be responsible for 100% of the costs if you are out of network without authorization.

With HMOs, you will select a Primary Care Physician (PCP); this will be the doctor responsible for managing your health care. You'll need to get referrals from this physician to see specialists, have lab work done, or have diagnostic testing performed. If you're considering an HMO plan, the single most important thing to do is make sure your primary doctor is 'in-network'. On the other hand, all Medicare Advantage plans cover you for emergency and urgently needed services when you're outside of your plan's service area, as long as you are in the United States. This means you can travel all over the country without worry.

PPOs are somewhat less common. They also have a network, but it's not an absolute requirement that you use their providers. However, you will usually pay lower out of pocket costs if you *do* use the providers in the preferred network. Where you see the biggest difference is usually with your annual out of pocket amount. The in-network cap is usually much lower than the out-of-network maximum, so again, check to be sure the doctors you need are in-network even in a PPO plan.

Whether you choose an HMO or PPO, the way you'll use your benefits is the same. Just like with Original Medicare, you'll be expected to pay a share of the costs when you use services or procedures. You can expect to encounter some or all of these costs:

- Medical Deductibles
- Medical Co-insurance
- Medical Co-payments
- Drug benefit Deductibles
- Drug benefit Co-insurance
- Drug benefit Co-payments

Not all plans have deductibles; in fact I would say most do not. You are much more likely to encounter a deductible with a PPO plan. However, with every Medicare Advantage plan, you can expect to pay co-payments or co-insurance. Generally, these out of pocket costs will be similar to what you would pay for Part B services under Original Medicare, or smaller. Remember, under Original Medicare, you pay 20% of the Medicare-approved cost. With Medicare Advantage plans, you will often pay a fixed co-pay. For instance, when you see your primary care provider, you might pay $5 to $30 per visit. This amount is often less than you would have paid under the terms of Original Medicare, but not substantially. The same goes for requirements such as lab work, x-rays, and specialist visits.

Medicare Advantage is most different in Part A hospital coverage. Remember that you would normally pay the Part A deductible ($1,484 for 2021) before Original Medicare begins covering your hospital benefits. With Medicare Advantage, you'll pay a smaller amount, but probably on a per-day basis. For example, you might find a daily co-payment of $295 for days one through seven; after this, the plan covers 100%. Using this example, you can see that for shorter hospital stays, you would save money under Medicare Advantage. On the other hand, if you stayed longer than five days, you would be paying slightly more with Medicare Advantage when compared to Original Medicare Part A.

Remember, the most important thing about Medicare Advantage—*you have a hard limit on your out of pocket expenses.* Even if these out of pocket costs add up, and you feel like you're paying a ton of co-pays and co-insurance, you know you're protected by that out of pocket cap. Again, this is totally different from what life is like under Original Medicare (unless you use Medigap).

The Cost For Medicare Advantage Coverage

So far, we've talked about how much you will spend on medical benefits and services if you have Medicare Advantage coverage. Let's talk about how much having Medicare Advantage coverage costs in the first place—I get a lot of questions about this.

You probably want to know, *How much will I have to pay for Medicare Advantage coverage?* The answer varies widely, based on several variables. These include:

- The population density of your county and state
- Whether you use an HMO or PPO
- The level of Extra Benefits provided by the plan
- The amount of competition in your market

For starters, the benefits provided by a Medicare Advantage plan, and their cost, are correlated to the population density of your community. The more rural your area, the higher your out of pocket maximum is likely to be, and the less likely you are to have a $0 premium option. Also, PPOs tend to be more expensive than HMO plans. Again, this is reflected in higher out of pocket caps, and also in higher monthly premiums. The same goes for Extra Benefits; a plan rich in Extra Benefits is more likely to have a higher monthly premium. Competition between insurance companies matters too, so smaller markets may have fewer Medicare Advantage plan choices; this often leads to higher premiums.

Before we jump in to how much your Medicare Advantage plan will cost, you need to understand one thing—you *must* keep paying your Part B premium. If you stop paying this, your Medicare Advantage plan coverage will be cancelled.

Besides your Part B premium, you might have an additional monthly premium for your Medicare Advantage Plan. Premiums vary widely; ranges from $0 per month to $70 per month are not uncommon. The average Medicare Advantage premium for 2021 is $21 per month—this includes people who pay $0 (Fuglesten Biniek et al., 2020).

QUESTION # 3 – How is it possible to have a $0 premium for Medicare Advantage?

ANSWER #3 – This is probably the most frequently asked question I get about Medicare Advantage plans. You already suspect the answer... nothing is truly 'free'. And that's a good hint, because CMS strictly prohibits the use of the term 'free' in any kind of Medicare Advantage marketing or presentation to the public. Do you remember that Medicare Advantage is an alternative to Original Medicare? Well, when you leave Original Medicare to join your Advantage plan, Original Medicare is no longer responsible for paying all of your medical expenses. So they pay your insurance company a fixed amount for every month you're in the plan. This payment is based on the average amount that a Medicare Beneficiary 'costs' the Medicare program. NOTE: this is a *basic* presentation of how the program works. There can be some costs reimbursed by Medicare to the insurance company. The main point is that Medicare Advantage plans receive money from Medicare to help pay for your medical costs.

Since you are paying taxes into Medicare as well as the Part B premium, you can see how your coverage is far from 'free'. But, when you use a $0 premium plan, what the insurance company is basically saying is, *we receive enough from Medicare to pay your claims and make a profit*. Once again, they may be 'making' money on you if they pay out less in claims than they receive from Medicare. But, you are at least getting the coverage, with an out of pocket maximum cap, for no additional premium, which is still a pretty good deal.

On the other hand, quite a few Medicare Advantage plans have a premium higher than $0. Sometimes this is the case for plans that have access to bigger, or more 'name brand' medical groups and hospitals. In other cases, there is just less competition, so premiums are higher than they would be otherwise.

Regardless of what the premium actually is, you need to consider what you're getting in exchange.

Usually 'what you are getting' includes prescription drug coverage. This is a key benefit, because the average monthly premium for a standalone Prescription Drug Plan in 2021 is $41 (Cubanski & Damico, 2020). In other words, most people in the country have access to Medicare Advantage plans with drug coverage at a $0 monthly premium. If you stay in Original Medicare and get a standalone drug plan, you would pay $41 per month on average.

QUESTION # 4 – Who is eligible for Medicare Advantage Plan coverage?

ANSWER #4 – This is an easy one—everyone who is eligible for Original Medicare Parts A and B is eligible for Medicare Advantage. Remember, you have to be enrolled in Part B to get Medicare Advantage, but as long as you are actively enrolled in Part B, and entitled to Part A, you can get Medicare Advantage coverage.

QUESTION # 5 – When can I sign up for Medicare Advantage?

ANSWER #5 – This depends on your circumstances. You will have a few options to get Medicare Advantage coverage, including:

- When you first enter Medicare (at age 65, or earlier, if that's how you qualify)
- During the Annual Enrollment Period (AEP), from October 15th to December 7th every year
- During a Special Election Period, if your circumstances change during the year

- When you enter Medicare, Part B, if you delayed your enrollment and now you are coming off employer or union coverage

If you're already enrolled in a Medicare Advantage plan, there are three times when you can change your coverage (switch from one plan to another):

- During AEP in the Fall (October 15th to December 7th)
- During a Special Election Period if you qualify for one
- During the Medicare Advantage Open Enrollment Period (MA-OEP, from January 1st to March 31st of each year)

This is important to remember—you *cannot* switch plans whenever you want. You must be in a valid election period, like AEP or MA-OEP.

Real World Case Study #1

Mr. M retired to Hilton Head Island after a career in education. He drew Social Security at age 65 and enrolled in Original Medicare. After a few years with this coverage, he decided to give Medicare Advantage a try. He was intrigued by the built-in drug coverage, the extra benefits available from the plan, and the fact that the monthly premium was affordable to him.

He chose a Medicare Advantage Prescription Drug plan that was structured as a PPO. He would have the freedom to use any doctor, but would pay less if he used the Preferred Providers listed in the plan. Mr. M is in good health and paid a few small co-payments to see the doctor when he had a cold, or to have a physical now and again. He preferred to pay a small monthly premium to maximize his cash flow. In a way, he was willing to save the premium money each month in exchange for the risk of paying a lot of co-payments and co-insurance if he had health problems.

Mr. M is a woodworker and makes custom furniture for clients. One day, he had an accident with one of his tools and suffered a severe injury to several of his fingers. He had to be rushed to the hospital. At the hospital, he received emergency surgery to re-attach his fingers to his hand. Thankfully, the surgery was a success. He needed several follow-up appointments and weeks of occupational therapy.

His total out of pocket costs for the hospital visit, surgery, follow-up visits, and therapy was just under $1,100. Though this is not an insignificant amount of money, he feels that his low Medicare Advantage plan premium has allowed him to save much more than this amount over the years. He is pleased that he chose Medicare Advantage.

Real World Case Study #2

Mr. T entered Medicare when he retired at age 65. His wife entered Medicare when she turned 65 a few months later. Their goal was to minimize premium payments while also limiting out of pocket expenses as much as possible. Given their budget requirement, Medicare Supplement Insurance was not considered for very long. Instead, they gravitated towards Medicare Advantage coverage.

They are both in good health, but with some underlying conditions. Both Mr. and Mrs. T take a number of medications for conditions like diabetes and arthritis. Some of these medications are quite expensive. They both enrolled in a Medicare Advantage plan after we confirmed that each of their doctors was in-network for the plan, and that their medications were also covered.

While they have been enrolled in their plans, they haven't experienced any medical emergencies. However, they do use their coverage quite frequently. For instance, they see their Primary Care Physician several times each year. They also see a specialist or two at least once per year. They pay small co-payments for these doctor's visits. They also pay small co-payments for various medical tests like bloodwork, x-rays, and MRIs.

They have had Medicare Advantage plan coverage for three years. Each year, they have paid, on average, $320 *combined* on co-payments and co-insurance. Considering their low premium payment, they are very satisfied with their decision to enroll in Medicare Advantage.

What To Remember:

- Medicare Advantage plans are an alternative to Original Medicare
- Most Medicare Advantage plans have network restrictions (especially HMOs)
- Medicare Advantage plans come with an annual Out of Pocket Maximum (OOPM) to protect you from out of control medical costs
- Many Medicare Advantage plans include prescription drug coverage (MAPD plans)

- You must continue to pay your Part B premium in order to have Medicare Advantage plan coverage

Chapter 6 – Enroll With Confidence

M

Congratulations! You now have all the information you need to make a coverage decision for Medicare Insurance. However, I know it can still seem like a lot of information to keep track of and process, so this last short section will ask you some questions that will get you moving in the right direction. Remember, you have three choices here:

- Stay in Original Medicare, and add a standalone Prescription Drug Plan
- Stay in Original Medicare, add Medicare Supplement Insurance, and a Prescription Drug Plan
- Enroll in a Medicare Advantage Drug Plan

While you can certainly use the first option, most people choose either Medicare Advantage or Medicare Supplement coverage to protect themselves from high out of pocket spending. Here are some questions to consider when choosing between Medigap and Medicare Advantage:

- Do you mind using a network of providers and relying on a Primary Care Physician for referrals to specialists?
- Do you plan to travel internationally often?
- Do you own homes in more than one state, or do you want to be able to see doctors and specialists anywhere in the country?

- Would you rather have a lower premium and pay small co-pays throughout the year, or pay a higher monthly premium with less out of pocket costs for every procedure/service you use?
- Can you afford a monthly premium of $90 to $170 per month in addition to your Part B premium?
- Based on your personal health history, and that of your relatives, are you particularly worried about high out of pocket spending for health-related conditions?

Consider Medicare Supplement Insurance if:

- You do *not* want to be restricted to networks and Primary Care Physicians
- You travel outside the US, or you split your time between two or more states

Medicare Supplement Insurance is also a good option if you hate the feeling of being 'nickel-and-dimed' and don't mind paying a higher monthly premium in exchange for lower out of pocket costs each time you use services and procedures. Also, give Medigap strong consideration if you have a family history of serious health issues, or if you have already dealt with them in your own life.

Consider Medicare Advantage Coverage if:

- You estimate that you're unlikely to incur too many co-payments due to heavy medical care usage each year

- You don't mind using a network of providers or relying on referrals from your Primary Care Physician

Give Medicare Advantage a long hard look if you would just like 'solid' coverage at an affordable price.

How To Get Your Medicare Insurance Coverage

Hopefully you feel equipped to make a smart decision on your Medicare Insurance coverage. You might ask, *How should I enroll in my plan?* I will tell you what I tell everyone I help with Medicare (even those who don't end up becoming a client): *Use an independent insurance agent.*

It can be tempting to rush in and call the insurance company of your choice, or go to the plan website and enroll all by yourself. Especially if you are someone who doesn't want to be 'sold' something, which I completely understand. However, if you've gone through this book and the free workbook (available at allofmedicare.com/enrollment-handbook), you have probably made a decision on your own. You're not being sold; you're making an informed choice. Now you just need to enroll in the *smartest way possible.*

Using an independent insurance agent is a great way to get your coverage, even if you already know the exact plan you want. An independent agent is, by definition, independent. They work with many insurance companies. This means that if your needs change (for instance, maybe your doctor changes medical groups and stops accepting your plan), an independent agent can help you enroll in a new plan, with a different insurance company. If you enroll directly with one insurance company, they will be no help in moving you to a different company.

For the same reason, an independent agent can help you research multiple plans with multiple carriers, and can get you quotes for each of them. They can help you easily decide which plan offers the best coverage for the price. An independent insurance agent can also do a lot of the heavy lifting when it comes to researching networks and formularies. I will say it again, it is *absolutely critical* that you make sure your doctor(s) and medication are covered by any Medicare Advantage or standalone Prescription Drug Plan you're considering. Let an independent agent help you with this important task.

With Medicare Insurance, you are dealing with two large bureaucracies—the federal government, and insurance companies. Neither is known for their TLC or personal attention to individuals. In other words, at some point in time, you're likely to have some kind of problem or concern with your coverage. A good independent agent will be there to help you get answers to your questions and advocate on your behalf, going to bat for you to make sure you get all the benefits you're entitled to.

Lastly, an independent insurance agent can do all of these things for you without costing you a single penny. Agents are paid by insurance companies. Your premium is exactly the same whether you use an agent or enroll directly with the insurance company. But, by using an independent agent, you gain access to a wealth of knowledge, and an advocate who can help you with your coverage for the rest of your life.

If you enjoyed or appreciated reading Mastering Medicare, maybe you'd like me to be your agent. I would be honored if you would consider me as your agent, and I will do everything I can to help you find and enroll in the plan that's right for your unique circumstances. Please email me at joe@allofmedicare.com, or call or text me on my cell phone at 858-248-0337. You can also reach out to me through my website, allofmedicare.com

Please Let Me Know What You Think

Thank you for reading Mastering Medicare! If you would like to share your thoughts about the book, or ask me a specific question, please email me at: joe@allofmedicare.com I would love to hear from you!

Honest Reviews Appreciated

If you found Mastering Medicare helpful, please consider leaving me a review wherever you bought it. You can also email me your review, which I might post on my website. My email address is joe@allofmedicare.com. Legitimate reviews will help others find this book and benefit from an unbiased primer in all things Medicare Insurance. Thank you!

More Free Resources From Me

If you would like more free educational resources, please visit my website at allofmedicare.com/medicare-education. If you have yet to download the free Mastering Medicare Handbook, please do so at allofmedicare.com/enrollment-handbook

Glossary

A selection of terms you should be familiar with. Note that definitions should be considered the authors opinion as to the easiest way to explain the term, i.e. a "working definition". Consult medicare.gov if you'd like a more detailed or official definition.

Annual Election Period (AEP) – An enrollment window from October 15th to December 7th of each year; everyone enrolled in Medicare can make changes to their coverage during this window.

Benefit Period – A period of time during which payment of the Part A deductible covers your hospital or skilled nursing facility stay. A benefit period begins with admission as an inpatient and ends when you haven't received care for the condition related to your admission for 60 consecutive days.

Cost Sharing – The amount you pay for a service or procedure, usually a co-payment or co-insurance amount.

Coverage Stage – For Part D drug plans (MAPD or standalone Prescription Drug Plans) only; one of five levels of cost sharing based on your total drug costs and the costs paid by your insurance company.

Deductible – An amount you must pay before your plan begins paying benefits.

Excess Charges – For Part B, these are amounts that some providers can charge above Medicare's prices. Not more than 15%.

Extra Benefits – Benefits that are not provided by Original Medicare Parts A or B. These benefits are generally offered by Medicare Advantage Plans in the form of coverage for vision, hearing, and dental, and in Medicare Supplement Insurance in the form of discounts.

Formulary – The official list of medications covered by a Part D drug plan.

Guaranteed Issue – An opportunity to enroll in a Medicare Supplement Insurance plan without answering health related questions; the insurance company must issue you a policy if you meet the criteria for Guaranteed Issue.

Health Maintenance Organization (HMO) – A health insurance plan that has a rigid network of providers and facilities; all care must be received from providers within the network.

Initial Coverage Election Period (ICEP) – A seven month enrollment window during which you can enroll in a Medicare Advantage plan. The ICEP is tied to your Medicare Part B enrollment period.

Initial Election Period (IEP) – A seven month enrollment window during which you can enroll in Medicare Parts A, B, and often, D. For most people, the IEP is centered on your 65th birthday.

Lifetime Reserve Days – Extra days that Medicare Part A will provide hospital benefits; you begin using these reserve days once you'd had a hospital stay of 90 days. You have a total of 90 Lifetime Reserve Days.

Medically Underwritten – Your acceptance in a Medicare Supplement plan is contingent on answering health questions when you don't qualify for Guaranteed Issue. If Medically Underwritten, you may be denied coverage, subject to pre-existing conditions exclusions, or charged a higher premium.

Medigap Open Enrollment Period – A six month enrollment window during which you are guaranteed acceptance into a Medicare Supplement Insurance plan. The six month period begins when you are 65 or older and enrolled in Part B.

Out Of Pocket Maximum (OOPM) – The most you can pay in one year for Medicare-approved medical expenses in a Medicare Advantage Plan or certain Medicare Supplement Insurance plans.

Palliative Care – Medical care that is designed to relieve pain and increase comfort during a terminal illness, once the decision is made to stop treating an illness for a cure.

Preferred Provider Organization (PPO) – A health insurance plan that offers lower cost-sharing for providers and facilities that are in the plan's network. You may use non-network providers, but you will pay higher cost-sharing.

Primary Care Provider (PCP) – A doctor, generally in an HMO plan, that you see for the general care of your health; your PCP refers you to specialists or facilities as they deem necessary.

Special Enrollment Period (SEP) – An enrollment opportunity that occurs due to an exceptional change in your circumstances; you may make changes to your Medicare coverage during an SEP.

Tier – A price level for medications in a Part D drug plan; the higher the tier, the higher your required cost-sharing.

References

Guo, J, Moon, M, 2017, March 31

Retrieved from

https://onlinelibrary.wiley.com/doi/full/10.1111/coep.1
2226

Cubanski, J, Damico, A, 2020, October 29

Retrieved from

https://www.kff.org/medicare/issue-brief/medicare-
part-d-a-first-look-at-medicare-prescription-drug-
plans-in-2021/

Fuglesten Biniek, J, Freed, M, Neuman, T, 2020,
October 29

Retrieved from

https://www.kff.org/medicare/issue-brief/medicare-
advantage-2021-spotlight-first-look/

Made in the USA
Las Vegas, NV
17 December 2021

38360643R00062